God's
PURPOSE
for MAN

God's PURPOSE *for* MAN

FROM CREATION TO HIS KINGDOM ON EARTH

CHARLES J. BELL SR.

XULON PRESS

Xulon Press
2301 Lucien Way #415
Maitland, FL 32751
407.339.4217
www.xulonpress.com

Unless otherwise indicated, Scripture quotations taken from the King James Version (KJV) – public domain

Printed in the United States of America.

Edited by Xulon Press

ISBN-13: 9781545638026

TABLE OF CONTENTS

About the Author ix

Introduction. 1

Chapter 1   The First Creation. 3

Chapter 2   The Second Creation 9

Chapter 3   Times of Noah 17

Chapter 4   In Search of a Nation 21

Chapter 5   God Sends Moses to Deliver Israel 27

Chapter 6   The Savior Comes 31

Chapter 7   What Must I Do to Be Saved? 43

Chapter 8   Now That I'm Saved, Now What? 47

Chapter 9   The Rapture—Judgment Seat of Christ 51

Chapter 10   The Tribulation. 57

Chapter 11   The Millennium 69

Chapter 12   God's Purpose Fulfilled 73

ABOUT THE AUTHOR

I remember when I was a child around ten or eleven years old; my mother had a special time of day when she would go into her room to pray. It was the room where she spent most of her time reading the Bible, playing her portable organ, and praying.

Sometimes she would make me come into the room and sit while she prayed, seemingly for everybody she knew. She would call out each person's name to God and ask God to bless them or help them go through a situation, and she would pray for the sick.

She would always pray for me and ask God to let her live until I became grown. That prayer was answered; she passed on my twenty-first birthday. Being as young as I was, my mind was not on praying, but more on going outside with the other kids in the neighborhood to play baseball.

One Sunday morning while I was at church with my mom, the choir sang so well, and I was touched by the words the preacher spoke about going to hell. When the preacher made the altar call, I was fearful, and my eyes flooded with tears that ran down my cheeks as he called for those who wanted to join the church. I walked down the aisle to the altar with tears flowing. The preacher looked at me and asked if I wanted to join the church and if I was willing to be governed by the rules and regulations of the church. I replied, "Yes."

He then asked the deacons and the congregation, "All in favor of this young man becoming a member of this church and a candidate for baptism, let it be known by saying 'aye.'" They all answered, "Aye." Then he asked the question, "All not in favor, say, 'nay.'" No one said, "Nay.' He shook my hand and welcomed me as a new member of the church, and the congregation gave me the right hand of fellowship by shaking my hand.

I thought at the time that I was saved and on my way to heaven, but nothing changed in my life. I had not heard anything about needing to be born again, repentance and forgiveness, a message on redemption, or anything about what Jesus Christ did for me. I did not know the significance of Jesus' blood or anything about His death and resurrection.

Many people today have joined the church but have never heard a message of redemption. They do not know what Jesus Christ did for them through His death, burial, and resurrection. Some are good people with good morals, good character, and good backgrounds. Some are faithful church-goers, singers in the choir, deacons, preachers, or Sunday school teachers, not fornicators or liars, who still have not been born again, yet they think they are on their way to heaven. What a catastrophe!

Shortly after my mother died on my twenty-first birthday, I visited a little storefront church where the preacher was preaching a message about the blood of Jesus and what the shedding of His blood did for all mankind.

I was convicted in my heart and confessed my sins to God, asking Jesus to save me and come into my heart and be the master of my life. At that moment, Christ came into my heart, and I received salvation. My whole life and mindset changed from that day forward.

I began to study God's Word, so I could learn more about Him. I attended Bible college and studied theology. I wanted to know why I was created and why the earth was created. I saw the condition of God's people, their lack of knowledge of His Word, and their lack of understanding of salvation.

I wanted to help people come to Christ and build the kingdom of God. What a tragedy and shame it would be for someone to go through their whole life thinking they have salvation, only to stand before God and hear Him say, "I never knew you; depart from me, ye that work iniquity" (Matthew 7:23).

For this reason, I am writing this book in the hope that someone will learn the truth about God's purpose for man—from creation to God's kingdom on earth.

I want people to know their need for salvation and the price and suffering Jesus paid for our redemption to bring mankind back into fellowship with God.

I pray that reading this book will be helpful and a blessing to each and every one who reads it.

God bless you all.

INTRODUCTION

GOD'S PURPOSE FOR MAN

For everything God does, He has a purpose before He does it. I believe when God was sitting on His throne in His heavenly kingdom, He had an eternal purpose and a plan to establish His heavenly kingdom on earth and have children on earth. He formed the earth to be inhabited (Isaiah 45:18).

After establishing a heavenly kingdom on earth, God would have His representative administrate over the earth, so it would be just like His heavenly kingdom in eternity.

In Matthew 6:10, Jesus was teaching His disciples how to pray, and in His teaching, He told them to pray, "Thy kingdom come, thy will be done in earth, as it is in heaven." This signified that God wanted earth to be just like heaven. His ultimate plan is to have a heavenly kingdom on earth, so mankind can enjoy His love and His glory for eternity on earth.

For God to fulfill His ultimate plan of establishing His heavenly kingdom on earth, He had to create a beginning. The first creation was the beginning of all creation and all things.

First, let us recognize who our God is. He is sovereign and has complete rule over all things. Nothing happens without His permissive or divine will. He is omnipotent: having all power over all things. God is also omniscient: having all knowledge of all things. He is omnipresent: in all places at the same time. What a great God we serve; His greatness is unsearchable.

1

Now let's see how God brings His purpose for man to pass, starting with eternity past.

The Bible has very limited information regarding what God did in eternity past. But as we study His Word, it is clear that He had a plan and a purpose for creation. The following is what I believe happened.

In eternity past, before there was a beginning, when there was no time, perhaps millions or even billions of years ago, God was dwelling in His heavenly kingdom and sitting on His throne in eternity.

There were no heavenly hosts—no angels, no cherubim, no seraphim—no beasts or any other beings. There was no world, no stars, no universe, no planets, and no earth. There was only God, the self-existent one, made up of three distinct persons: God the Father, God the Son, and God the Holy Spirit. No one else existed, but God has always existed. To fulfill His ultimate purpose, He decided to create a beginning.

CHAPTER 1

THE FIRST CREATION

B efore there was a beginning, there was God. God existed before the beginning. God is greater than the beginning because He created the beginning. The beginning came out of God.

Before the beginning, nothing existed. God created the beginning out of nothing. When God spoke, space came into existence. Let us take a look at God's creations.

Genesis 1:1-2 tell us, "In the beginning God created the heaven and the earth. And the earth was without form and void; and darkness was upon the face of the deep. And the Spirit of God moved upon the face of the waters."

These two verses of Scripture are two of the most interesting verses in the Bible. From an outward appearance, they don't seem to tell us very much. But when you search them out, they tell us quite a bit, including how sin entered the universe and why the world is in such chaotic condition today. Let us walk through these two verses and see what I believe happened.

Verse 1 says God created the heaven and the earth. Many theologians agree that when God created the heaven and the earth, He also created all the angelic beings, such as the cherubim and seraphim, the beasts, and every creature He wanted in heaven, including Lucifer, who became Satan.

I agree with them. As Psalm 33:6 tells us, "By the word of the Lord were the heavens made; and all the host of them by the breath of his mouth." That was the end of the first creation. So, everything God created in verse 1 was perfect and good. God has never created anything that was not good. But in verse 2, we read that "the earth was *without form and void*, and darkness was upon the face of the deep."

Something drastic happened between verse 1, where everything God created was perfect and good, and verse 2, where everything was without form and void. The phrase "without form and void" comes from the Hebrew word *toho vabohu*, which means "desolate, waste, chaotic, and ruined."

Now what could have happened between Verse 1, where the earth was perfect and good, and verse 2, where the earth was desolate, waste, chaotic and ruined? I believe it was sin that caused the chaos on earth. Let us explore God's Word and see how I believe it happened.

Lucifer in Eden

When God created the earth, He created it to be inhabited. It was His first step toward having a heavenly kingdom on earth. Isaiah 45:18 tells us, "For thus saith the Lord that created the heaven; God himself that formed the earth and made it, he hath established it to be inhabited. I am the Lord and there is none else." So, we know God created the earth to be inhabited.

After God created the earth, God placed Lucifer, the angel, in Eden, the garden of God, as ruler of the earth. He was God's representative and administrator on earth so that earth would be as His heavenly kingdom in eternity. Lucifer was the anointed cherub that covereth, meaning that he had exalted privilege as an angel guarding God's interest. He was set apart for God's divine purpose to fulfill God's eternal plan on earth.

God gave Lucifer a certain amount of power and authority and also gave him free will. With free will, Lucifer had the ability to obey or to reject God's will. Lucifer's job was to defend, protect, and guard God's interest on earth.

Lucifer was the leader of the angels in worship and praise, who glorified the almighty God. God had given Lucifer dominion over the earth, and all the angelic beings adored Lucifer. Seemingly, Lucifer had everything he could want. He was talented, had authority and prestige, and was very beautiful. What more could he have wanted? Still, Lucifer wanted more. His beauty, talent, and authority went to his head, and his pride made him want to be equal with God, his creator. Lucifer wanted to receive the praise that only God deserved.

Lucifer became uplifted and exalted with pride, or developed what I call the "big head." Like so many people today who receive power or prestige, Lucifer's head swelled, and he forgot who he was and who gave him the power. One of the reasons behind Lucifer's pride was of his beauty.

In Ezekiel 28:13 and Isaiah 14:12-14, God sent His prophets to address Satan, who was working through the kings of Tyre and Babylon, and He describes the way Lucifer was while he was in Eden, the Garden of God.

Let us see what God said about Lucifer in Ezekiel 28:13. "Thou hast been in Eden the garden of God: every precious stone was thy covering, the sardius, topaz, and the diamond, the beryl, the onyx, and the jasper, the sapphire, the emerald, and the carbuncle, and gold: the workmanship of thy tabrets and of thy pipes was prepared in thee in the day that thou was created." These nine jewels describe Lucifer's great beauty.

"Thou art the anointed cherub that covereth; and I have set thee so: Thou was upon the holy mountain of God: Thou has walked up and down in the midst of the stones of fire" (Ezekiel 28:14). God allowed Lucifer to set up his throne on the holy mountain of God.

"Thou was perfect in thy ways from the day that thou was created; till iniquity was found in thee. . . Thine heart was lifted up because of thy beauty, thou hast corrupted thy wisdom by reason of thy brightness, I will cast thee to the ground, and I will lay thee before kings, that they may behold thee" (Ezekiel 28:15, 17).

Look at what God had entrusted into the hands of Lucifer. The holy mountain of God is where Lucifer had his throne on earth, yet Lucifer was greedy and wanted more. God tested him, and he failed the test, so God couldn't trust him anymore. Lucifer's pride had caused him to fall. Solomon said it well in Proverbs 16:18: "Pride goeth before destruction, and an haughty spirit before a fall." That is what happened to Lucifer.

Lucifer had become narcissistic, thinking he was "all that" and that everything revolved around him. Listen to how he was described in Isaiah 14:13-14: "For thou hast said in thine heart, I will ascend into heaven, I will exalt my throne above the stars of God; I will sit also upon the mount of the congregation, in the side of the north: I will ascend above the heights of the clouds; I will be like the Most High." Notice how Lucifer used the term "I will." He used it five times while he was planning a rebellion against God. It was a clear indication that he was full of pride. God always has a way to humble someone who is full of pride. Proverbs 6:17 tells us that God even hates a proud look.

The Fall of Lucifer

Lucifer was dissatisfied with the authority to rule over the earth that God had given him; he wanted more. He decided he wanted to be equal with God; so, he organized all the angels that were faithful to him, and they rose up against the almighty God. One third of the angels in heaven agreed with Lucifer's mindset to rebel and overthrow God and take over God's kingdom. Look at the influence Lucifer had over the angels. Their rebellion against God failed, and they were all cast back down to earth.

Lucifer was viciously mad at God; he planned to destroy and disrupt God's plan for a heaven on earth. Isaiah 14:12 tells us, "How art thou fallen from heaven, O Lucifer, son of the morning! How art thou cut down to the ground which didst weaken the nations." In Luke 10:18, Jesus said, "I beheld Satan as lightning fall from heaven." How foolish are the things pride will cause a person to do? Don't let pride cause you to disobey God.

Lucifer, the beautiful angel whom God had trusted and to whom He had given so much power and authority, became Satan. With Satan's fall came the meaning of Genesis 1:2: "And the earth was without form and void, and darkness was upon the face of deep." The fall of Lucifer and his angels brought darkness upon the earth. As Jeremiah 4:23 tells us, "I beheld the earth, and, lo, it was without form, and void; and the heavens, and they had no light."

God flooded the earth with water, and all life and vegetation were destroyed. The earth was no longer as He had created it; it was ruined, and darkness was all over.

Sin had now entered the universe, and Lucifer and his fallen angels became evil spirits and demons. There was no space for them to repent for their rebellion against God. God had judged them and sentenced them to the lake of fire, where they would spend eternity. They are now waiting until God executes His judgment upon them on the last day. Until then, they are going to and fro, seeking to deceive God's people and destroy as many as they can in order to stop God's eternal plan.

For the present, God is still allowing Satan to come before Him to accuse the brethren, as he did in Job 1:6. "Now there was a day when the sons of God came to present themselves before the Lord, and Satan came also among them."

Satan accused God of having a hedge around Job, and if God removed the hedge from around Job, he would make Job curse God to His face. Satan is out to get you, but he cannot do more than God allows.

CHAPTER 2

THE SECOND CREATION

During the first creation, Satan and his angels failed in their rebellion against God as they tried to take over His throne in eternity. As a result, God kicked them out of heaven and back to earth, where they became demons and evil spirits. After that, I believe God decided to make a second creation; only this time, it would be much different from the first creation.

Genesis 1:26 tells us, "And God said, let us make man in our own image, after our likeness: and let him have dominion over the fish of the sea, and over the fowl of the air, and over the cattle, and over all the earth, and over every creeping thing that creepeth upon the earth." This passage tells us that God restored earth to its original beauty, including light, vegetation, and animal life. When God said, "Let us make man," He was referring to the divine trinity of the Father, Son, and Holy Spirit. When He said, "And in our image and likeness," He was referring to our outward form. In His creation of man, God also gave man free will—the ability to choose to obey Him or reject Him.

God placed Adam in the Garden of Eden and gave him a wife as a help meet so that Adam would have companionship and would not be lonely. The garden must have been beautiful, with its fruit trees, vegetables, herbs, grass, and streams flowing through it to water the garden. Everything was beautiful and pleasant to the eyes.

Adam had all he could ever want in his day. He had a healthy body, peace of mind, a beautiful wife, joy in his heart, and unlimited access to God. He had dominion over the fowls of the air, the animals of the ground, and the fish of the sea. God even brought every animal to Adam so that he could give them each a name. Adam had rule over everything as far as the eye could see. Most importantly, he had fellowship with God. What more could Adam have wanted?

After God placed Adam and Eve in the garden, He wanted them to have something to do, so He gave them a job. "I want you to dress the garden and to keep it," He said, and He told them, "I want you to replenish the earth." "Replenish the earth" indicates that there had been life on earth before Adam.

God also gave Adam one commandment. "Of every tree of the garden thou mayest freely eat: But of the tree of the knowledge of good and evil, thou shalt not eat of it: for in the day that thou eatest thereof thou shalt surely die" (Genesis 2:17). Can you imagine having only one commandment to obey? Remember, God had given Adam free will, with the choice to obey or disobey.

The Fall of Adam

Now Satan heard God give Adam the command not to eat from the tree of the knowledge of good and evil because he would surely die if he did. So, Satan began to scheme and plan to get Adam to disobey God's command.

One day as Adam and Eve were walking through the garden admiring God's glorious garden and beautiful fruit trees, along came Satan's tool, the serpent, who approached Eve in his cunning and deceitful manner. Notice that he didn't approach Adam; he approached Eve instead.

The serpent asked Eve a question, even though he already knew the answer. "Hath God said, ye shall not eat of every tree of the garden?" The serpent was trying to plant a seed of doubt in Eve's mind. Eve replied to the serpent that God had said, "We may eat of the fruit of the trees of the garden: But of the fruit of the tree which is in the midst of the garden God hath said ye shall not eat of it, neither shall ye touch it, lest ye die" (Genesis 3:2-3). The serpent told Eve, "God knows you won't surely die. He doesn't want you to be as gods and know good and evil." Notice that this serpent was not like the ordinary serpents we see today. This serpent was unique in that it was able to talk, carry on an intelligent conversation, and understand everything God had spoken to Adam (Genesis 3:1-5). The serpent was actually Satan in a serpent's form. The serpent was the most subtle, cunning, and deceptive creature in the garden, who I believe walked upright, as later he was cursed upon his belly (Genesis 3:14).

After the serpent told Eve that she wouldn't die if she ate of the fruit, can you imagine how he may have taken a bite of the fruit to prove to Eve that she wouldn't die? When she saw that he didn't die, the serpent probably told her, "See, I told you that you wouldn't die. You can see that it didn't kill me." After seeing that the serpent didn't die, Eve was convinced that he was telling the truth. She saw that the fruit was pleasant to the eyes, took it, and ate of it. When she saw that nothing happened to her, she was even more convinced that the serpent had told her the truth. She then turned to Adam and offered a bite to him because it tasted good, and she hadn't died.

Adam saw that nothing happened to Eve, and because he had free will, he willingly took of the forbidden fruit and ate of it. Immediately, the eyes of both Adam and Eve were opened because Adam had sinned, and now sin had entered the earth. Suddenly, they saw that they were naked and no longer had glorified bodies.

When Eve ate of the fruit, nothing happened because God had given the command to Adam and not to Eve. When Adam ate of the fruit, he disobeyed God's command, and from that day until today, all mankind was born in sin, separated from God, and in need of salvation.

Now that the eyes of Adam and Eve were opened, they knew good and evil and were ashamed of their nakedness, so they sewed fig leaves together into garments to cover themselves. They realized they had sinned against God and had become spiritually separated from Him. This began the cycle of physical death for Adam and all of mankind that followed.

Because of Adam's sin, all of creation was affected and in need of redemption. Sickness came into the world along with all manner of disease, as well as murder, fear, strife, maliciousness, adultery, fornication, hatred, abusiveness, evil thoughts, gambling problems, alcohol problems, drug problems, sex problems, lust, pride, financial problems, and every sin under the sun. Now mankind and all creation needed to be redeemed. Everything God had given to Adam, He gave back to Satan.

While Adam and Eve were in the garden, "they heard the voice of the Lord God walking in the garden in the cool of the day: and Adam and his wife hid themselves from the presence of the Lord God amongst the trees of the garden. And the Lord God called unto Adam and said unto him, Where art thou?" (Genesis 3:8-9)

"And he said, I heard thy voice in the garden, and I was afraid, because I was naked; and I hid myself. And God said, Who told thee that thou wast naked? Hast thou eaten of the tree, whereof I commanded thee that thou shouldest not eat? And the man said, The woman whom thou gavest to be with me, she gave me of the tree, and I did eat" (Genesis 3:10-12).

Notice how Adam started making excuses and using the blame game to accuse God and Eve. Notice that he said, "Lord, You're the one who gave this woman to me," as if telling the Lord that if He hadn't given her to him, this wouldn't have happened. Adam told the Lord Eve was the one who made him eat. People are still the same today, not taking responsibility for their mistakes.

That is the way that so many people respond when they are caught red-handed doing wrong. They try to justify their wrongdoing by making excuses instead of accepting their responsibility.

"And the Lord God said unto the woman, what is this that thou hast done? And the woman said, the serpent beguiled me, and I did eat" (Genesis 3:13). Like Adam, Eve also pushed the blame on someone else instead of admitting that what she had done was wrong. But God always goes to the source of the problem.

"And the Lord God said unto the serpent, because thou hast done this, thou art cursed above all cattle, and above every beast of the field; upon thy belly shalt thou go, and dust shalt thou eat all the days of the life" (Genesis 3:14).

God first put a curse on the serpent. No longer would the serpent be able to walk upright, but now he had to crawl on his belly all the days of his life. No more speech nor cunning. This shows the effects of sin. Man went from eternal life and glory to being spiritually separated from God, having physical death and disease, along with all manner of problems—because of sin. The serpent fell from being one of God's most beautiful creations to being a loathsome snake.

God Promises Man Hope

God told the serpent, "And I will put enmity between thee and the woman; and between thy seed and her seed; it shall bruise thy head, and thou shalt bruise his heel" (Genesis 3:15). This is the first promise God made to redeem man, and it began the seed that would bring Jesus Christ. There will be a great division between Satan and Jesus Christ.

Unto the woman, He said, "I will greatly multiply thy sorrow and thy conception; in sorrow thou shalt bring forth children; and thy desire shall be to thy husband, and he shall rule over thee" (Genesis 3:16). God let the woman know she would have pain during childbirth and would be subject to her husband.

And unto Adam, He said, "Because thou hast hearkened unto the voice of thy wife, and hast eaten of the tree, of which I commanded thee saying thou shalt not eat of it; cursed is the ground for thy sake; in sorrow shalt thou eat of it all the days of thy life"

(Genesis 3:17). Because Adam rebelled against God and listened to his wife, Eve, he now had to work by the sweat of his brow to make a living from the land.

"Unto Adam also and to his wife did the Lord God make coats of skins, and clothed them" (Genesis 3:21). When God created man, man had a glorified body, and his nakedness was not shown. But because of Adam's sin, his body was exposed as naked, and blood had to be shed for God to make a covering for man's sin before man could have fellowship with God.

Adam Expelled from the Garden

"And the Lord God said, Behold, the man is become as one of us to know good and evil: and now, lest he put forth his hand, and take also of the tree of life, and eat, and live forever: therefore the Lord God sent him forth from the garden of Eden, to till the ground from whence he was taken: So he drove out the man; and he placed at the east of the garden of Eden cherubims, and a flaming sword which turned every way, to keep the way of the tree of life" (Genesis 3:22-24).

God had to put angelic beings at the east gate of the garden to keep Adam and Eve from trying to re-enter the garden. If Adam and Eve had returned to the garden and eaten from the tree of life, they would have lived forever in sin. With Adam's fall, Satan believed he had stopped the plan of God to establish a heavenly kingdom on earth.

Adam and all of creation must now wait until God redeems man and all creation through His Son Jesus' death, burial, and resurrection.

Now that Adam and Eve have been expelled from the Garden of Eden, they faced an unknown world and saw themselves in a strange place that they had never seen before and knew nothing about. They were spiritually separated from God, and physical death was certain to come as God promised; they had to deal with the consequences that would come upon them because of their sin. Adam had given back to Satan everything God had given to him, which was the rule and dominion over earth. Satan is now the ruler of this world and the prince of darkness, and all mankind has become a slave to sin until they accept Jesus Christ as their Savior.

Fear came upon Adam, and many of the creatures he had named and once had dominion over became his enemy. The lion and the tiger could kill him; the serpent would bite him. No longer was he in the beautiful Garden of Eden in which God had placed him, a land of good and plenty. No longer did he have unlimited access to God. No longer was he in a place where there has never been darkness, for he had lived in the light of God. Now he had to fight for survival, for food, for shelter. He would experience cold and heat, danger and darkness, and hard work to survive.

He had to face the consequences of sin and darkness. Sin always has a consequence. Adam was in a helpless situation and was the cause of all creation to fall, but God had a plan, which had been prepared specifically for this day before the foundation of the world.

Adam had fallen and lost connection with God. Satan believed he has destroyed God's plan to have a heavenly kingdom on earth. But God, who is omniscient and knows all things, knew before the foundation of the world that Satan was going to use his cunning ways to deceive Eve and cause Adam to sin. This is when God starts the process of redemption to restore man to full fellowship with Him. Adam and Eve had three sons, Cain, Abel, and Seth. There was jealousy in the family, and Cain committed the first murder by killing his brother Abel. Seth was born, and his descendants began a line of redemption down to Noah.

CHAPTER 3

TIMES OF NOAH

During the time of Noah, the world was wicked, violent, and evil and was committing all manner of sin. The very imagination of man was continuously evil. The world was so wicked that God repented that He had created man. He decided that He would no longer allow man to exist. Genesis 6:7 tells us, "And the LORD said, I will destroy man whom I have created from the face of the earth; both man, and beast, and the creeping thing, and the fowls of the air; for it repenteth me that I have made them." God found favor in Noah because he lived a righteous life and had demonstrated his faith in God. Noah had a wife and three sons, Japheth, Ham, and Shem.

God spoke to Noah and told him that He was going to destroy man and everything on earth and flood the earth with water. Because of Noah's righteousness, however, God promised to save Noah and his family, as well as two of every animal on earth. He instructed Noah to build an ark. He gave Noah the dimensions for the ark and told him the materials he must use. Noah followed God's instructions. The ark was to be 450 feet long, 75 feet wide, and 45 feet high. It took Noah 120 years to build the ark.

Can you imagine the ridicule Noah went through from those around him? Building an ark on dry land, miles from the sea; plus, it had never rained on earth before. The people must have thought he was insane. They laughed and made jokes about him, but he continued to obey God. Noah warned the people what was going to happen, but because they were so wicked, they refused to take heed and rejected what God had said. When Noah finished the ark, God told him to take his family and enter it. Then it began to rain, and the door was shut. The flood was something man had never seen. At first, I imagine, it was very puzzling to them to see drops of rain. The drops kept falling and became heavier, the sky darkened, and the thunder began to roar. The rain poured down harder, and great fear came upon the people. They ran to the ark and cried out to Noah, "Save us and let us come in!" But it was too late.

For forty days and forty nights, the rain fell until the whole earth was flooded. All of mankind, vegetation, and all life on earth perished except for Noah and his wife, their children, and their children's wives. God saved the eight people and all the animals that were on the ark.

After the flood was over, God placed a rainbow in the sky and made a covenant with Noah as a reminder that He would never again destroy the earth by water. Every time you see a rainbow in the sky, it is a reminder of God's covenant.

When Noah and his family left the ark, the first thing he did was build an altar and give praise to God for his deliverance. He and his family were the only people on the face of the earth. To continue his plan for the redemption of man, God instructed Noah to multiply and replenish the earth and gave them authority to eat living creatures as food. Noah began to work the soil and planted a vineyard with grapes. He made wine out of the grapes, and one day, he got drunk from the wine and was naked. His son Ham saw him naked and laughed at him. The other two sons, Japheth and Shem, refused to look at their father naked and covered him up. When Noah discovered what had happened, he cursed his son Ham to a lifetime of servitude.

Noah's son Ham had a son named Cush, and Cush had a son named Nimrod. Nimrod was a very interesting man. He was a mighty hunter and warrior. His kingdom began in Babel, and he founded other great cities such as Nineveh. But he would not honor God. At the time, the whole world spoke one language. Nimrod wanted people to worship him and decided to build a tower that would reach all the way to heaven.

God saw that the people were of one accord and had one language. He said, "Let us go down, and there confound their language, that they may not understand one another's speech" (Genesis 11:7). God went down and confused their language, so they could not understand each other and scattered them throughout the whole earth. From that time on, people were scattered throughout the earth and spoke different languages. They began to form and build their own nations.

CHAPTER 4

IN SEARCH OF A NATION

With people scattered around the world, God began to look for those whom He could use to form a nation through which He would bring salvation to the world. That nation would be a light and an example to other nations, and through that nation, all the earth would be blessed.

God saw Abram, a man of faith and a descendant of Noah's son Shem, dwelling in the land of Haran. God spoke to Abram, who was seventy-five years old, and told him to leave his country and go to a land that He would show him. "I will make thee a great nation, and I will bless thee, and make thy name great, and thou shalt be a blessing" (Genesis 12:2). Having this promise from God, Abram gave up his pagan beliefs and by faith took his family and left his home in Haran. He started on the road to the land where God would lead him. Abram and his family went into the land of Canaan, and the Lord appeared unto him and said, "Unto thy seed will I give this land" (Genesis 12:7).

Now there was a famine in the region, and Abram took his family and went to Egypt, where there was food. Sarai, Abram's wife, was childless, nor could she bear children. Thus, she gave her Egyptian handmaid, Hagar, a slave girl, to Abram, and Hagar bore Abram a son, whom they named Ishmael. This birth created problems for Sarai. Hagar wanted her son to get the inheritance from Abram, but Sarai did not want that. God saw Sarai's desire for a son.

When Abram was ninety-nine years old and Sarai was ninety years old, God spoke to Abram and changed his name to Abraham. "For a father of many nations have I made thee" (Genesis 12:5). He also changed Sarai's name to Sarah. And He told Abraham, "Sarah thy wife shall bear thee a son indeed; and thou shalt call his name Isaac: and I will establish my covenant with him for an everlasting covenant, and with his seed after him" (Genesis 17:19). God told Abraham that this time next year Isaac would be born, and He would establish His covenant with Isaac.

When Isaac was born as the child of God's promise, Sarah now wanted Isaac to receive Abraham's inheritance instead of Ishmael. Abraham had to send Ishmael away to Egypt with his mother, Hagar. This decision insured Isaac's undisputed inheritance.

Later, Isaac and his wife, Rebekah, had two sons, Esau and Jacob. The younger son, Jacob, took advantage of his brother's hunger and convinced Esau to trade his birthright for some stew. Later, Rebekah and Jacob deceived Isaac, and Isaac gave Jacob the blessing that belonged to Esau. This created a division between Esau and Jacob and caused Jacob to run and escape to avoid Esau killing him. For twenty years, Jacob was on the run from his family. He never saw his mother alive again.

One night, the angel of the Lord appeared unto Jacob, and he wrestled with the angel and said that he wouldn't let the angel go until he blessed him. The angel pulled Jacob's thigh out of joint, and Jacob still refused to let him go.

And the angel said unto Jacob, "What is thy name?" and he said, "Jacob." And the angel said to Jacob, "Thy name shall be called no more Jacob, but Israel: for as a prince hast thou power with God and with men, and hast prevailed" (Genesis 32:27-28). This is how the nation of Israel got its name. God is building the nation he promised.

Jacob had twelve sons, who became the twelve tribes of Israel. Now one of Jacob's sons was named Joseph. He favored Joseph over the other brothers and, as a result, he almost destroyed the family. His favoritism caused the other brothers to show envy, strife, and hatred toward Joseph. They also had malice against their brother because he told them his dreams, which stated that his brothers one day would bow down to him. That made them hate Joseph more. Whenever a parent shows favoritism to one child over another, it causes confusion and discord in the family.

One day, Joseph's brothers were out feeding the flock, and Jacob sent Joseph down to see how they were doing. When they saw him coming they devised a plan to kill him and make it look as if an animal had killed him. When Joseph arrived, they threw him in a pit, but when they saw a caravan of Midianites coming, they decided it was better to sell him instead of leaving him to die. They pulled Joseph out of the pit and sold him to the Midianites, but they told their father that an animal had killed him. The Midianites took Joseph to the slave market, where he was sold to an Egyptian officer named Potiphar.

Joseph was a smart young slave, and Potiphar found him to be faithful and trustworthy. He placed Joseph in charge over the affairs of his household. With Joseph in charge, Potiphar prospered greatly.

He had a beautiful wife who lusted after Joseph and even tried to lure him into bed, but Joseph refused. He remained faithful to God and to Potiphar. He refused to lower himself and go against God's will, so ran out, leaving his coat behind, to avoid committing sin with Potiphar's wife. Potiphar's wife was so upset by Joseph's rejection that she went to her husband and lied to him. She told him Joseph tried to have relations with her.

Potiphar got very angry and had Joseph put in prison for something he didn't do. For years, Joseph was in prison, but he found favor with the prison keeper and was put in charge of the other prisoners. When a person does the right thing, God will give that person favor.

While Joseph was in prison, he met two of Pharaoh's officers who had been put in prison and were awaiting judgement. One was a chief baker, and the other was a chief butler. Pharaoh had imprisoned them for suspicion of wrongdoing. One day, they both had a dream they did not understand and asked Joseph to interpret the dreams for them. Joseph interpreted both dreams. A few days later, just as Joseph had interpreted, the chief chef was hanged, and the chief butler was set free and restored to his former position. Joseph asked the chief butler to remember him when he was with Pharaoh.

A few years later, Pharaoh had two dreams that greatly disturbed him. He sent for magicians and wise men to interpret the dreams, but they could not. The chief butler remembered how Joseph had interpreted his dreams while he was in prison, so he advised Pharaoh of a man in prison who was skillful in interpreting dreams. Pharaoh had Joseph brought to him to interpret his dreams.

Joseph interpreted both dreams for Pharaoh. The first dream meant that Egypt would have seven years of plenty. After that, they would have seven years of famine. He told Pharaoh that he should start preparing before this came to pass. Pharaoh was so impressed with Joseph that he made him head of the granaries and second-in-command over all of Egypt. Those who wait on the Lord shall renew their strength. When you obey God, you will be rewarded.

After seven years of plenty in Egypt, the famine Joseph had predicted came and affected the whole known world. People from other countries had to come to Egypt to get grain and corn to survive. The famine hit hard in Canaan, where Joseph's father, Jacob, and his family lived. Jacob instructed his sons to go to Egypt to get grain to keep them from starving.

When Joseph's brothers arrived in Egypt, they had to stand before their brother in order to buy grain. They did not recognize Joseph because he had become a man of great authority and was second-in-command of all of Egypt. But Joseph immediately recognized his brothers. When his brothers had to bow to him, he remembered that the dreams God had shown him years earlier had come to pass. Joseph tested his brothers in several ways before he revealed his identity to them. Through his love and kindness, he forgave his brothers for what they had done to him. What they meant for evil, God made it turn out for the good. Joseph restored good relations with his brothers and gave them grain and sent them back to Canaan to get his father, Jacob, and they all settled in Egypt (Genesis 45:4-8).

After Joseph's death, another Pharaoh came into power in Egypt, and he feared the Hebrews would overtake his kingdom because they had become so great in number. Therefore, Pharaoh enslaved the Hebrews, and they remained in captivity as slaves in Egypt for four hundred years.

CHAPTER 5

GOD SENDS MOSES TO DELIVER ISRAEL

Israel had now been in captivity in Egypt for four hundred years. The taskmasters of Egypt had been cruel and overbearing to the children of Israel. The children of Israel had suffered long and hard and began to cry out to the almighty God for their deliverance. God heard their cry. Pharaoh had heard that the Hebrews were expecting a savior to come and rescue them out of bondage. Pharaoh ordered all Hebrew baby boys to be drowned in the Nile River.

But God had a future plan for baby Moses. Moses' mother hid him in a waterproof basket and put him on the Nile River. Pharaoh's daughter found him and raised him as a member of the royal family. When Moses was forty years old, he saw an Egyptian beating up one of the Hebrew slaves. Moses intervened and killed the Egyptian and hid his body in the sand. Afraid that Pharaoh would have him executed, Moses fled Egypt to Midian and lived there for forty years. There, he found his wife.

When God got ready to deliver Israel out of captivity in Egypt, He spoke to Moses and instructed him to go down to Egypt and tell Pharaoh to "let My people go" (Exodus 9:1). But Moses was afraid and began to make excuses to God as to why he couldn't go. He told God that his speech was not eloquent, and that Pharaoh would not listen to him. God told Moses to go and tell Pharaoh that "I AM" had sent him.

Moses obeyed God and went to Egypt. He took his brother, Aaron, as his spokesman, and they stood boldly before Pharaoh and told him that "I AM" had sent him to tell him to let His people go so that they could worship Him. Pharaoh refused. Time and time again, Moses went to Pharaoh and told him to let God's people go, but each time, Pharaoh refused. So, God hardened Pharaoh's heart because he refused and sent plagues upon the people of Egypt.

God plagued the water and turned it to blood. All the rivers turned to blood. The fish died, and the water had such a foul odor that people couldn't drink it. God smote the land with frogs, and that irritated the people. God also smote the land with lice and stinging flies. God smote the cattle, and all the cattle of Egypt died, causing a shortage of meat in the land.

God afflicted man and beast with boils and sent hail and fire upon the people of Egypt, and they suffered greatly. With all of that, Pharaoh, with his hard heart, would not let God's people go.

"And the Lord said unto Moses, Go in unto Pharaoh: for I have hardened his heart, and the heart of his servants, that I might shew these my signs before him: And that thou mayest tell in the ears of thy son, and of thy son's son, what things I have wrought in Egypt, and my signs which I have done among them; that ye may know how that I am the Lord" (Exodus 10:1-2).

Moses and Aaron went back to Pharaoh and told him, "Thus saith the Lord God of the Hebrews, How long wilt thou refuse to humble thyself before me? Let my people go, that they may serve me" (Exodus 10:3). Pharaoh refused, and God sent locust upon the earth, filling the houses of Pharaoh's servants and the houses of the Egyptians. And the locust ate every herb and the fruit of the trees.

God spoke again to Moses to stretch forth his hand to heaven, and darkness came over the land of Egypt. It was so dark that the people could not see one another, but the children of Israel had light in their dwellings. It was dark for three days, and no one moved from their places. Can you imagine darkness so dark that you can't see your hand in front of you?

God was ready to deliver the children of Israel out of their captivity. But none of the plagues moved Pharaoh's heart to let God's people go, so He would use blood. God instructed Moses to speak to the congregation of Israel and tell every man to take a lamb without spot or blemish, a male of the first year from the sheep or goats.

They were to kill the lamb or goat, take the blood, and apply it over the upper doorpost and on the side post of their houses. God said, "I will pass through the land of Egypt when I see the blood, and I will pass over you." He said that she would pass through Egypt at midnight and go through the midst of Egypt, and all the firstborn in the land of Egypt would die, from the firstborn of Pharaoh to the firstborn of the maid servants to the firstborn of the beasts. Through the blood of the lamb and goats, God redeemed the children of Israel out of captivity in Egypt. Without the shedding of blood, there would be no redemption. Through this event, God showed Israel the power in the blood. Pharaoh finally gave in to God's great power and let God's people go. Exodus 12:37 tells us about six hundred thousand on foot that were men, beside children.

God Sets a Standard for Israel (The Law)

After God had delivered Israel out of captivity in Egypt, they came to the wilderness of Sinai, and He gave Moses the Law—the standard by which the people were to live. Before the Law came, sin was not known as sin. The Law that God gave was the Ten Commandments (Exodus 20:3-17). They are as follows:

1. Thou shalt have no other gods before me.
2. Thou shalt not make unto thee any graven images.
3. Thou shalt not take the name of the Lord thy God in vain.

4. Remember the Sabbath day to keep it holy.
5. Honor thy father and thy mother.
6. Thou shalt not kill.
7. Thou shalt not commit adultery.
8. Thou shalt not steal.
9. Thou shalt not bear false witness against thy neighbor.
10. Thou shalt not covet.

God chose Israel to be a special people unto Himself—a people for His own possession. Deuteronomy 7:6 tells us, "For thou art an holy people unto the Lord thy God: the Lord thy God hath chosen thee to be a special people unto himself, above all people there are upon the face of the earth."

Moses led the people out of Egypt to the edge of the promised land before he died. God chose Joshua to carry His people over into the promised land. This land will one day be the place where God will set up His kingdom on earth and fulfill His purpose for man. According to Genesis 15:18 God made a covenant with Abraham, saying, "Unto thy seed have I given this land, from the river of Egypt unto the great river, the river Euphrates." This was confirmed in Joshua 1:3-4, when God spoke to Joshua and said, "Every place that the sole of your foot shall tread upon, that have I given unto you, as I said unto Moses. From the wilderness and this Lebanon even unto the great river, the river Euphrates, all the land of the Hittites, and unto the great sea toward the going down of the sun, shall be your coast." Inside this land is Israel and the great city of Jerusalem. During the millennium period, Jesus will reign from His throne in Jerusalem, the capital of Israel.

CHAPTER 6

THE SAVIOR COMES

God first promised a savior when Adam and Eve were in the Garden of Eden as He spoke to the serpent in Genesis 3:15, saying, "And I will put enmity between thee and the woman, and between thy seed and her seed; it shall bruise thy head, and thou shalt bruise his heel." God was letting Satan know he was going to send a savior for man. That savior would be His Son, Jesus Christ, who would shed His blood for the redemption of man. There would be a division between Satan and Jesus, but in the end, Jesus would come out ahead by crushing Satan.

When Jesus was born in Bethlehem, Satan immediately began a plan to destroy Him to prevent God's plan of redemption from coming to pass. Satan used King Herod to gather all the chief priests and scribes of the people together and demanded that they find where Jesus was born with the pretense that he wanted to worship Jesus.

However, Herod's real plan was to destroy Jesus. When he couldn't find Jesus, Herod ordered all the children two years old or younger in Bethlehem to be slain. But God was aware of Herod's plan to destroy Jesus and had an angel of the Lord appear unto Joseph in a dream to tell him to take his child, Jesus, and the child's mother, Mary, and flee into Egypt until He brought word that it was safe for them to return to Israel. Herod later died.

God instructed Joseph to return to Israel with his family, Mary, and Jesus.

When Jesus began His ministry, He went to John the Baptist to be baptized. After He was baptized, God spoke from heaven and said, "This is my beloved Son in whom I am well pleased" (Matthew 3:17). Jesus was then led of the Spirit into the wilderness to be tempted by the devil. He fasted for forty days and forty nights and was very hungry afterward.

When Satan saw that Jesus was hungry, he took it as an opportunity to tempt Jesus while He was at his weakest point. This is how Satan deceives God's people. He'll wait until you are at your lowest point then begin his attack on you. Let us observe how Jesus handled Satan.

Satan asked Jesus, "If thou be the Son of God, command these stones to be made bread." Satan used the term *if* as though there were doubts that Jesus was God's Son. Jesus said, "It is written, Man shall not live by bread alone, but by every word that proceeded out of the mouth of God" (Matthew 4:4). You should always use the Word of God on the devil when he tempts you because there is power in God's Word.

Satan was persistent. He didn't stop there but tried again, only this time, in a different way. He took Jesus into the holy city and set him on the pinnacle of the temple. The devil began to misquote Scripture verses from Psalm 91:11-12 and said, "If thou be the Son of God, cast thyself down: for it is written, He shall give his angels charge concerning thee: and in their hands they shall bear thee up, lest any time thou dash thy foot against a stone." This is the reason to know God's Word, for Satan will use half-truths, as he did with Eve in the garden, to make her go against God.

Again, Jesus used the Word of God against Satan and quoted Deuteronomy 6:16, saying, "It is written again, Ye shall not tempt the Lord your God." Three times, Satan tried to get Jesus to bow down and worship him. He took Jesus to a very high mountain and showed Him all the kingdoms of the world, and said, "All of this will I give to you if you will bow down and worship me." Satan had the power to do this. Remember, when God created the earth, He first put Satan—then called Lucifer—in Eden and gave him charge and dominion over everything. But Satan lost it when he unsuccessfully tried to overthrow God and was cast back to earth. He regained this dominion when Adam sinned and turned everything God had given him back to Satan. That is why he told Jesus that he would give it to him if Jesus bowed down and worshipped him.

Again, Jesus used the Word on Satan: "Get thee hence, Satan: for it is written, Thou shalt worship the Lord thy God, and him only shalt thou serve" (Deuteronomy 6:13). Satan left him alone for a season. The apostle James said, "Resist the devil, and he will flee from you" (James 4:7). You must have the courage to say no when you are tempted. That's how you can stand up against the devil.

The Message Jesus Preached

Jesus started His ministry by going from synagogue to synagogue throughout the land and preached a new message to the people. He had a tremendous task ahead of Him. He had to change the mindset of the Jews concerning the Mosaic Law, letting them know that He did not come to destroy the Law but to fulfill it. Most Jews were set in their ways regarding the Law, but Jesus came to teach them a new and better way. So, the message Jesus taught was about the kingdom of God, a message they had never heard before.

This message stated that a literal government would be established on earth at the second coming of Christ. In order to prepare them to enter into the kingdom of God, Jesus taught them how they must live their lives.

In the Sermon on the Mount in Matthew chapters 5–7, Christ set forth the perfect standard of righteousness that the Law demands. He demonstrated that all men are sinners, falling short of God's divine standard, and that salvation by works of the Law was an impossibility.

Jesus taught two important messages: the importance of forgiveness and the true meaning of love. Even today, people go for years holding grudges against someone who has done something to them or said something about them. They even say that they'll never forgive that person as long as they live. Just think what would have happened if Jesus hadn't forgiven you for things that you did against others or when you made a mistake. Where would you be today? Someone may have borrowed money from you without paying you back, and every time you see that person, your spirit rises up in you. But if you forgive, it frees your spirit, and you can honestly treat them as though nothing had ever happened. Someone may have said something bad about you, and you may feel like getting even. This feeling is wrong. Jesus told us to forgive others for what they have done to us just as we would want forgiveness for the things we have done. The kicker to this point is that Jesus also said that if we do not forgive others for what they do to us, neither will He forgive us (Matthew 6:15). Nothing anyone has done wrong against you is worth your holding on to; it only causes grudges, hatred, malice, and strife. Let it go and free yourself. Forgiveness is not just for the one you forgive; it's also for you because it frees you as well as them.

The other message that Jesus taught was the importance of having love. "A new commandment I give unto you, That ye love one another; as I have loved you" (John 13:34). Jesus gave them no choice when it came to love. He commanded them to love. He told them that love was the only way others would know they were His disciples. "By this shall all men know that ye are my disciples, if ye have love one to another" (John 13:34). Love is a Christian identification mark. A person can talk like a Christian and act like a Christian, but if they don't have love, they are like a "tinkling cymbal" (1 Corinthians 13:1).

If you are a Christian, your love will come forth in your life-style. You will be kind to others even if they are not kind to you. You won't hold iniquity against others in your heart. You won't be easily provoked by others, and you won't think evil toward others. Love will give people the benefit of the doubt. Remember how much God loved us—so much that He gave His Son for our salvation.

Jesus Voluntarily Gave Up His Life for You

The time was near when Jesus would face the difficult task of giving His life for the saving of the world. He took His three closest disciples, Peter, James and John, with Him to a place called Gethsemane to pray. He asked them to wait while He went up to pray.

He was very sorrowful as He fell on His face and cried out to God His Father and asked, "O my Father, if it be possible, let this cup pass from me: never the less not as I will, but as thou wilt" (Matthew 26:39). As Jesus looked into this bitter cup, all the sins of the world flashed before Him. He saw all the hatred, murder, strife, malice, lust, jealousy, and all manner of sin in the cup. He saw disease and sickness in the cup. He saw trials, disappointments, and discouragement in the cup.

His fate was so horrible that Jesus asked God to take it away if that was possible. But God would not take it away, for if man was to be saved, His demand had to be met; blood had to be shed. The only blood that met God's standard was the blood of Jesus.

Three times Jesus went up to pray, and twice He asked God to take it away. But on the third time, His mind was made up: He knew that He must take the cup and lay down His life so that man could be saved. He said, "O my Father, if this cup may not pass away from me, except I drink it, thy will be done" (Matthew 26:42). Sometimes we go through trials and feel as if we can't make it through. God told Paul that His grace was sufficient to take him through any trials.

Jesus looked beyond the faults of man and saw the need of the world. "Greater love hath no man than this, that a man lay down his life for his friends" (John 15:13). Jesus proved His love for all mankind. "Therefore, doth my Father love me, because I lay down my life, that I might take it again. No man taketh it from me, but I lay it down of myself. I have power to lay it down, and I have power to take it again. This commandment have I received of my Father" (John 10:17-18). Man did not have the power to take Jesus' life. He volunteered and gave it up Himself for our salvation.

Jesus Is Crucified

As it came closer for Jesus Christ to be crucified, Satan stirred up the high priest and scribes, Pharisees and the elders of the people, and they assembled together and conspired a plan to kill Jesus. Judas, a disciple of Jesus, approached the priests and made an agreement with them to betray Jesus for thirty pieces of silver. He also agreed to show them where Jesus could be found so they could bind and arrest Him. For a little money, Judas sacrificed his soul and betrayed Jesus. "For the love of money is the root of all evil" (I Timothy 6:10).

When they found Jesus, they arrested Him and took Him to the high priest, but Caiaphas had Jesus taken to the judgment hall where He stood before Pilate. After Pilate had questioned Jesus, he said that he could find no fault in this man and would have Jesus go free, but the people cried out not to set Jesus free. Instead, they wanted the murderous Barabbas to go free. Satan had their minds so messed up that they would rather let a murderer go free than a faultless Jesus.

Pilate, being afraid that the people would complain to Caesar about him, gave instructions for Jesus to be scourged, thinking this would soften the hearts of the Jews toward Jesus. Under Jewish law, forty stripes were the maximum amount they could give Him (Deuteronomy 25:3). Scourging was a public punishment that was used to cause terrible pain and agony by beating the person with a whip. The whip was three-thronged and weighted with jagged pieces of metal to make each blow extremely painful and tear open the skin.

They took the clothes off Jesus, so His back was bare, and they gave Him forty stripes minus one (2 Corinthians 11:24). Each lash on His back tore open His skin and ripped it, causing blood to gush out and run down Jesus' back. This was so painful, but Jesus never said a word. Scourging was usually reserved for slaves or criminals that had done the most terrible crimes, but Jesus was not guilty—as Pilate had said, "I find no fault in this man" (Luke 23:4).

After Jesus had been scourged, the soldiers platted a crown of thorns and crushed it down on His head causing excruciating pain, and the blood came streaming down His face. Pilate had them put on Him a purple robe, which represented royalty and kingship, in hopes that this would melt the hearts of the people, so he could let Jesus go free.

The chief priest and the officers began to cry out, "Crucify Him! Crucify Him!" Crucifixion was a Roman form of execution. After Pilate heard these words, he became more fearful and delivered Jesus to them to be crucified. Crucifixion was so dreaded that it was unlawful for a Roman citizen to be crucified. It was the cruelest form of death known to man.

Roman soldiers made a heavy cross and forced Jesus to bear the cross and carry it to a place called Golgotha. They spit on Jesus and called Him names as He struggled to carry the heavy cross. When He got to Golgotha—a place they called "the skull"—with His body half naked, they laid Him down on the cross and stretched His arms so far until they came out of their sockets, causing Jesus tremendous pain.

After they had stretched His arms out of proportion, they took spikes and nailed His hands and His feet to the cross. The pain was excruciating, but Jesus never complained and never said a word. His body was so torn and disfigured that He didn't look like a man. They raised the cross in the air and dropped it in a hole with a loud thump, causing Him even more pain.

Now two thieves hung on crosses next to Jesus, one on each side of Him. One of the thieves said, "If thou be Christ, save thyself and us." But the other thief answered him, saying, "Dost not thou fear God, seeing that you are in the same condemnation? . . . We receive the due reward of our deeds: but this man hath done nothing amiss." He then said to Jesus, "Lord, remember me when thou comest into thy kingdom. And Jesus said unto him, Verily I say unto thee, Today shalt thou be with me in paradise" (Luke 23:39-43).

And darkness fell over the land from noon until three p.m. And great fear came among the people, and some realized this must be the Son of God. When Jesus became thirsty, they filled a sponge with vinegar and put it upon hyssop (a plant that grows six feet) and put it to Jesus' mouth. After Jesus tasted the vinegar, He said, "It is finished" (John 19:30).

What was finished? Jesus had finished all the suffering that was required of Him to redeem man. The division between the Jews and Gentiles had been broken. He had broken down the middle wall of partition to make Jews and Gentiles one body in Christ. Now we have personal access to God, whereas before we had no personal access to God. Now we can go to God ourselves instead of the priest going for us. "For through him we both have access by one spirit unto the Father" (Ephesians 2:18). By His death, we now have salvation for all. "In whom we have redemption through his blood, the forgiveness of sins, according to the riches of his grace" (Ephesians 1:7). And when Jesus cried out with a loud voice, He said, "Father, into thy hands I commend my spirit: and having said thus he gave up the ghost" (Luke 23:44). A soldier took a spear and pierced Jesus in the side, and blood and water came out. Jesus had died.

Jesus in the Grave

Jesus had died, and He had paid the price for man's salvation through the shedding of His blood. But He still had to face a major task, and that was the grave. The Word of God tells us, "By which also he went and preached unto spirits in prison" (1 Peter 3:19). These spirits in prison were the spirits of the believers that had died before but had hoped and believed that a Savior would one day come for their redemption (1 Peter 3:18-19).

I believe all the old patriots, prophets, and believers who were looking for that blessed hope were waiting on Jesus' coming. But they were locked up in prison, and Satan had the only key to the prison. In captivity was Adam, the father of the human race. Abraham, Isaac and Jacob were in the grave in captivity. Isaiah, the prophet who was in the grave, had foretold of the horrible torture Jesus was going to experience. He said, "He was wounded for our transgressions, he was bruised for our iniquities; the chastisement of our peace was upon him; and with his stripes we are healed" (Isaiah 53:5).

David, Israel's greatest king, was also in the grave, locked in captivity. David had written in Psalm 16:10, "For thou wilt not leave my soul in hell." Job was there. He had asked God a question: "If a man die, shall he live again? All the days of my appointed time will I wait, till my change come" (Job 14:14). The thief who hung on the cross next to Jesus was there when Jesus told him, "Today shalt thou be with me in paradise" (Luke 23:43).

I imagine Satan knew that Jesus had died and was at the gates of hell, waiting to receive him. He remembered how Lazarus had died and was at the gates of hell; but Jesus had raised him from the dead, depriving Satan of putting Lazarus in captivity. Satan, the captain of death and the prince of hell, and all his demons were waiting and prepared for Jesus' arrival. They were excited because no one except Lazarus had ever been to the gates of hell and escaped. I believe they were determined to hold Jesus in the grave. They knew that if they could hold Jesus in the grave, His death and the shedding of His blood to save all mankind would be in vain.

I imagine when Jesus went into the grave, suddenly, a great light shone in the darkness of the grave, and Satan and all the demons began to tremble with great fear. It was Jesus. I believe he cried out with a loud voice as of thunder and a mighty rushing wind and said, "Lift up the gates and let the King of glory come in!" Satan and his demons trembled even the more, wondering if Jesus would cast them into the everlasting lake of fire. He cried out again, "Open up the gates and let the King of glory come in!"

The gates were opened, and Jesus Christ, the King of glory, entered the grave, trampled on death, and put to flight the horrid powers of darkness and death. He broke down the prison from top to bottom and released all the saints that were bound. I believe he saw Job and said, "I heard your cry when you asked the question, 'If a man die, shall he live again? All the days of my appointed time will I wait, till my change come'" (Job 14:14). And Jesus said, "I am the resurrection and the life: he that believeth in me though he were dead, yet shall ye live" (John 11:25).

I believe Jesus stretched forth His hand and told the saints to come to Him. He ascended from hell, and all the saints were with Him. "And the graves were opened; and many bodies of the saints which slept arose, and came out of the graves after his resurrection, and went into the holy city, and appeared unto many" (Matthew 27:52-53). If Jesus had not risen from the dead and come out of the grave, His death would have been in vain, and everybody would still be held in Satan's captivity and would be lost without a Savior. Thank God for Jesus. All the glory belongs to Him.

Jesus Returns to Heaven

Before Jesus was crucified, He had told the Pharisees and the scribes of the sign of the prophet Jonah, "For as Jonah was three days and three nights in the whale's belly; so shall the Son of man be three days and three nights in the heart of the earth" (Matthew 12:40). He was letting them know that the Son of man would rise again on the third day. So, early in the morning on the third day, when it was still dark, Mary Magdalene went to the sepulchre and saw that the stone had been removed, and Jesus was not there. She ran and told Peter and John what she had seen, and they came and verified that Jesus was not there. Peter and John returned home and left Mary by the sepulcher, weeping. While she was weeping, she saw two angels in white sitting beside it, and they asked her why she was weeping. She replied to them, "They have taken away my Lord."

When she turned back, she saw Jesus standing there but didn't recognize Him. Then Jesus said, "Mary," and she looked again and realized that it was Jesus. She ran with excitement to touch Him, but He told her, "Touch me not; for I am not yet ascended to my Father: but go to my brethren, and say unto them, I ascend unto my Father, and your Father; and to my God, and your God" (John 20:17). There are several views by Theologians as to why Jesus told Mary not to touch him. The view that I understand to be true is that Jesus was acting as the High Priest fulfilling the Day of Atonement in Leviticus 16, in which the blood of animals only covered the sins of Israel but did not take them away. When Jesus sacrificed His blood, His sacrifice took away all the sins of man, all the way back to Adam. Jesus' blood sacrifice covered all sins—past, present, future—for all mankind. As the High Priest, he could not be touched by man because He had not yet ascended to heaven to present the sacred blood to God so that man's salvation would be secure. Jesus had to make a blood report to His Father and present the sacred blood in heaven.

Jesus told Mary to go and tell the others that He had to ascend to His Father. After Jesus had made His blood report to the Father, He returned and met with His disciples: "And, behold, I send the promise of my Father upon you: but tarry ye in the city of Jerusalem until ye be endued with power from on high" (Luke 24:49). The promise the Father sent was the Holy Ghost, who would comfort them and come to live inside them to lead and guide them.

And Jesus "led them out as far as to Bethany, and he lifted up his hands, and blessed them." He told them He would return quickly. "And it came to pass, while he blessed them, he was parted from them, and carried up into heaven. And they worshipped him, and returned to Jerusalem with great joy," praising the almighty God (Luke 24:50-53).

Jesus came and shed His blood and met God's demands that would restore man to fellowship with Him by accepting and believing in His shed blood. Jesus took away from Satan all that Adam had given him when he sinned. Jesus made a way for man to live in the kingdom of God for eternity.

Now let us see what mankind must do to reach the kingdom of God.

CHAPTER 7

WHAT MUST I DO TO BE SAVED?

Romans 5:19 tells us, "For as by one man's disobedience many were made sinners, so by the obedience of one shall many be made righteous." Since Adam sinned against God, all mankind has been born in sin. Adam received a sin nature that he inherited from Satan, and that sin nature was inherited by all man; therefore, we were all born sinners. That sin nature is the spirit of Satan and the root cause of man committing sin. Man cannot help himself because Satan has power over him. But when Jesus came and shed His blood as payment for our redemption, all who would believe on him from their heart and accept Him as the Son of God and what He has done for them would be saved and would receive a new nature on the inside, which is the Nature of God. They would then have power to resist the devil.

Many "good" people live in the world today. They have good morals, take care of their families, and don't give anybody any problems. They don't curse or commit adultery or fornication. They don't smoke or gamble, don't do drugs or even drink alcohol. They go to church every Sunday; they teach Sunday school, sing in the choir, serve on the usher board or deacon board. They preach the Word to others. They pay their bills on time. They are really good people, and yet they are sinners, if they have not accepted Jesus as their Savior. Why? Because Jesus said, "You must be born again."

The apostle Paul said, "All have sinned and come short of the glory of God" (Romans 3:23). No matter how good a person is, everybody since Adam who has chosen to sin has been born in sin and is in need of salvation to make it into God's kingdom. Paul said, "For by grace are ye saved through faith; and that not of yourselves: it is the gift of God" (Ephesians 2:8). We cannot do anything to save ourselves. We don't deserve salvation—we can't earn it, we can't buy it, and we can't work for it. It is purely a gift only God can give.

Jesus said, "For God so loved the world, that he gave his only begotten son, that whosoever believeth in him should not perish, but have everlasting life" (John 3:16). Only what Jesus did through the shedding of His blood and through His death, burial, and resurrection saves us. That was the provision that God made for sinful man by giving up His Son to be sacrificed for the sins of the whole world. What love the Father has for us!

In the Bible, Nicodemus was a Pharisee and a ruler of the Jews. He was a man of influence and great authority, and he lived strictly according to the Law of Moses. Nicodemus had heard about Jesus and had witnessed some of the miracles Jesus had performed. Out of curiosity, Nicodemus wanted to know more about Jesus, so he went to Jesus by night and told Him that no man could do the miracles He had done except if God be with him.

Jesus perceived what Nicodemus really wanted to know and answered him, "Verily, verily, I say unto thee, except a man be born again, he cannot see the kingdom of God" (John 3:3). The answer Jesus gave was confusing to Nicodemus, for he couldn't understand how a man could enter again into his mother's womb. Jesus made it plain: "Verily, verily, I say unto thee, except a man be born of water and of the spirit, he cannot enter into the kingdom of God" (John 3:5).

Nicodemus understood being born of water because it was a Jewish term for a physical birth or being born of the flesh. For example, every child that is born naturally lies in water inside an amniotic sac in their mother's womb before he is born. When the mother's "water breaks," that child comes forth in birth. This is the fleshly birth or being born of water.

Being born of the Spirit comes from above. This birth comes only through faith—by a person believing and accepting that Jesus Christ is the Son of God who came and gave His life through the shedding of His blood, was buried and raised again on the third day, and later ascended back to heaven. You cannot be born again without accepting Jesus Christ and what He has done for you.

Paul said, "That if thou shalt confess with thy mouth the Lord Jesus, and shalt believe in thine heart that God hath raised him from the dead, thou shalt be saved" (Romans 10:9). You must believe in Jesus, for as He said, "I am the way, the truth, and the life: no man cometh unto the Father, but by me" (John 14:6). You cannot get to God except through Jesus Christ. You cannot bypass Jesus. There is no other way.

In Philippians 2:9-11 Paul said, "Wherefore God also hath highly exalted him, and given him a name which is above every name: that at the name of Jesus, every knee should bow, of things in heaven, and things in earth, and things under the earth; and that every tongue should confess that Jesus Christ is Lord, to the glory of God the Father."

Acts 4:12 tells us, "Neither is there salvation in any other: for there is none other name under heaven given among men, whereby we must be saved." Jesus gave everybody an open invitation to come to Him, and He would give them rest. "Come unto me, all ye that labour, and are heavy laden, and I will give you rest. Take my yoke upon you, and learn of me; for I am meek and lowly in heart, and ye shall find rest unto your souls. For my yoke is easy and my burden is light" (Matthew 11:28-30). It doesn't matter what your circumstance is or what you have done in life.

No problem is too big or too small that Jesus cannot handle. Take your trials to Jesus. Let Him know about your problems because He's the ultimate problem-solver.

God told Isaiah, "Come now, and let us reason together. . . though your sins be as scarlet, they shall be as white as snow; though they be red like crimson, they shall be as wool" (Isaiah 1:18). This is the reason Jesus came: to save us and reconnect us to God so that we can enter His kingdom and live for eternity.

When you come to God with a sincere heart, believe in your heart and confess with your mouth that Jesus Christ has been raised from the dead, and accept Him as your Savior, you shall receive salvation (Romans 10:9). You then become a member of the royal family of God, and you cannot lose your salvation because your spirit is sealed. Your salvation is secure in the hand of Jesus, and no one can take you out of His hands (Ephesians 1:13). As Jesus said, "And I give unto them eternal life; and they shall never perish, neither shall any man pluck them out of my hand. My father, which gave them me, is greater than all; and no man can pluck them out of my Father's hand. I and my Father are one" (John 10:28-30). You are on your way to the kingdom of God to spend eternity with Him. Praise the almighty God!

CHAPTER 8

NOW THAT I'M
SAVED, NOW WHAT?

N ow that you've received salvation and are sealed by the
Holy Spirit, this new position in Christ does not mean that
you won't have problems. Your journey will not be easy. This is
just the beginning. Many people believe that when they receive
salvation, everything will be fine and dandy and their problems
will be over. That line of thinking is totally wrong. After you get
salvation, that's when Satan will do all he can to make your life
miserable so that you won't enjoy your salvation or all the ben-
efits that God has in store for you.

Remember that when you receive salvation, you won't be
fighting against flesh and blood; instead, you'll be standing up
against the trickery and wiles of the devil. You'll be wrestling
against principalities, against powers, against the rulers of the
darkness of this world, and against wickedness in high places
(Ephesians 6:12). Satan and his demons will be your enemy.
Remember that. He will try to make things hard for you. He will
bring trials and all manner of problems and try to keep you out
of the will of God.

But Jesus made the truth plain for a new convert when He said,
"Take my yoke upon you, and learn of me" (Matthew 11:29). That
is such an important statement. The first thing we need to do is

learn about Jesus. Learn about His character, His power, His love, His peace, His forgiveness, His patience, and His longsuffering.

How do we learn about Jesus? We learn about Him by reading and obeying His Word. The Word contains the thoughts and mind of God. We need the Word to clean up our lives. Jesus said, "Now ye are clean through the word which I have spoken unto you" (John 15:3).

You can use the Word when going through temptations. When Jesus had fasted forty days and forty nights in the wilderness, He was very hungry when He came out. The first thing He encountered after He came out of the wilderness was the devil trying to tempt Him. Satan said to Jesus, "If thou be the Son of God, command these stones to be made bread" (Matthew 4:13). Jesus put the devil in his place by quoting the Word: "It is written, Man shall not live by bread alone, but by every word that proceedeth out of the mouth of God (Matthew 4:4). The Word will put the enemy to flight. It takes the Word of God to clean up your life. Obeying God's Word will allow you to live a victorious life. God said, "My people are destroyed for lack of knowledge" (Hosea 4:6). You need the Word to learn about God.

The Word of God will teach you all you need to know about how to live a Christian life. Remember: Jesus is the Word. John 1:1 tells us, "In the beginning was the Word, and the Word was with God, and the Word was God." Learn it and practice it.

Learning about Jesus is a process. You don't learn it all in a day. That process is called sanctification. Jesus said, "Sanctify them through thy truth; thy word is truth" (John 17:17). Learning His Word and obeying Him are the keys to learning about Jesus. David once said, "Thy word have I hid in my heart that I might not sin against thee" (Psalm 119:11). As noted above, the Word contains the mind and thoughts of God. This is the first thing you need to learn.

Many people get confused when others explain to them what they must give up to be saved. Some people tell new converts that they must give up smoking, drinking, unsaved friends, gambling, and many other things. But Jesus tells us to come as we are. Bring everything to Him, and He'll work it out. That's the reason you need Jesus: you can't do it on your own.

The Word also teaches us that we must have faith. "The just shall live by faith" (Romans 1:17). We cannot please God without faith. Hebrews 11:6 tells us, "But without faith it is impossible to please him: for he that cometh to God must believe that he is, and that he is a rewarder of them that diligently seek him."

What is faith? In Hebrews 11:1 we read, "Now faith is the substance of things hoped for, the evidence of things not seen."

How do we get faith? To get faith, we must first get the Word because without the Word, there is no faith. It is the Word that produces faith. The apostle Paul said, "So then faith cometh by hearing, and hearing by the Word of God" (Romans 10:17). When you hear the Word of God, that Word produces the confidence or the substance you need to believe that the promise of God or the things hoped for are true. When you act upon the Word by obeying it, it produces the evidence of things which were once not seen but are now seen and have become a reality.

When God spoke to Abram to leave his father's house and go to where God would lead him, Abram did not hesitate to obey. The spoken word God gave produced the confidence Abram needed to leave his home. When Abram acted upon that word, it produced the results God had promised.

You must depend on God's Word to deal with the daily problems that you will face in these perilous times. Things are getting worse every day. Hurricanes, fires, murders, and racial and economic problems all indicate that Satan is gathering all his forces together to come against man as he has never done because he knows his time is not long. Nobody knows when Jesus is coming, but we do know He is coming soon to take the church out in the rapture.

CHAPTER 9

THE RAPTURE—THE JUDGMENT SEAT OF CHRIST

I remember one day I was sitting in my office at home and listening to Andre Crouch as he was singing, "Soon and very soon, we are going to see the King." The song was so powerful that it brought tears of joy to my eyes. As I fantasized the joy of being in glory with the Lord, it reminded me that one day very soon, if we believe in Him as our Savior, we are going to see the King.

I heard the Word of God say that no man knows the day or the hour when the Son of man will come (Matthew 24:36). It will be sudden and unexpected, but one thing is certain: we must all be ready when He comes. It could be early in the morning when people are eating breakfast or getting ready to go to work. We could be getting the children ready to go to school, or it may be at noon or during the midnight hour. We could be watching television, at a sporting event, in church praising God, or on the beach relaxing. We don't know when He's coming, but He is.

I am talking about when Jesus comes in midair to receive the church—His saints—and takes them to heaven to live and receive their rewards at the judgment seat of Christ for the works they did on earth after they became a Christian. This is called the rapture, meaning "being caught up." Oh, what a joyous day that will be for all of God's children!

The Word of God describes this glorious day in this way: "For the Lord himself shall descend from heaven with a shout, with the voice of the archangel, and with the trump of God: and the dead in Christ shall rise first: Then we which are alive and remain shall be caught up together with them in the clouds, to meet the Lord in the air: and so shall we ever be with the Lord" (1 Thessalonians 4:16-17). Two people may be sitting at a table; one may be caught up and the other left behind. People may be sleeping in bed; one caught up, the other left behind. Some may even be in church, with some caught up and others left behind. This would be tragic for the ones left behind.

Can you imagine a shout so powerful that it will awaken saints who have been asleep for ages? It will happen so quickly— as the apostle Paul said, "In a moment, in the twinkling of an eye at the last trump" (1 Corinthians 15:52). If you're not ready to go back with the Lord when He comes, you won't have time to get ready. So, get ready now.

The dead in Christ shall rise first; the ashes of their bodies will be changed from corruptible to incorruptible and raised together with their spirits, and they'll be changed from mortal to immortality. The bodies of the saints that are alive will be changed, and they will be caught up to meet the others in the air. We will all meet the Lord in the air. What a glorious day that will be!

Judgement Seat of Christ

After the rapture has taken place and we reach heaven, we will all stand before the judgement seat of Christ. The Lord Jesus Christ will be the judge. 2 Corinthians 5:10 tells us, "For we must all appear before the judgement seat of Christ; that everyone may receive the things done in his body, according to that he hath done, whether it be good or bad." This is not a judgement for sins. This judgement only pertains to Christians, because Jesus has already redeemed us from sins. The purpose of this judgement is to evaluate the way we lived our Christian lives, and the quality of Christian service while we were on earth. Apostle Paul tells us in 1 Corinthians 3:13-15, "Every man's work shall be made manifest: for the day shall declare it, because it shall be revealed by fire; and the fire shall try every man's work of what sort it is. If any man's work abide which he hath built thereupon, he shall receive a reward. If any man's work shall be burned, he shall suffer loss: but he himself shall be saved; yet so as by fire."

One thing Jesus is going to judge in our Christian service is our deeds, or what we do—whether it be good or bad. Do we do good to impress others, or do we do good because it is right? In Matthew 6:1, Jesus said, "Take heed that ye do not your alms before men, to be seen of them: otherwise ye have no reward of your Father which is in heaven."

Jesus will judge the words we say. He told us in Matthew 12:36, "But I say unto you, that every idle word that men shall speak, they shall give account thereof in the day of judgement." Be careful what you say about others because Jesus also told us in Matthew 12:37, "For by thy words thou shalt be justified, and by thy words thou shalt be condemned."

Jesus is going to judge our secrets—things that only we know about. Apostle Paul told us in Romans 2:16, "In the day when God shall judge the secrets of men by Jesus Christ according to my gospel."

Jesus will also judge our faithfulness, our dependability, and our trustworthiness. It is so important that a Christian be faithful. Apostle Paul said in I Corinthians 4:2, "Moreover it is required in stewards, that a man be found faithful."

I want to reiterate that when you stand before the judgement seat of Christ, the judgement is not about whether or not you are saved. You were not saved by works, you were saved by Grace. "For by grace are ye saved through faith; and that not of yourselves: it is the gift of God" (Ephesians 2:8). Even if your works may be burned, you shall be saved (1 Corinthians 3:15).

In your everyday life, you go to a job and work hard, and sometimes you work overtime. At the end of the week, you expect to be rewarded for the work you have done. I don't know of anyone who works without expecting a reward. When Jesus was on the cross, He looked toward the coming reward. "...who for the joy that was set before him endured the cross, despising the shame, and is set down at the right hand of the throne of God" (Hebrews 12:2).

Rewards are earned by your works on earth and how you helped build the kingdom of God. Paul describes building on Christ's foundation as gold, silver, and precious stones. If a man builds on the foundation of faith in Christ, the works will follow. He is faithful, just, prayerful, and obedient to the Word of the Lord, keeping his life pure unto the Lord and helping others get into the kingdom. When his life is tested by fire through temptations, trials, and sufferings, he passes the test by trusting God. When his works are tried by fire, they don't burn. The ones who build on the foundation of wood, hay, and straw are the ones whose works don't have eternal value and are burned. They are saved but don't receive a reward.

Crowns

We know that we do not have to do works to be saved to go to heaven. Ephesians 2:8 tells us, "For by grace are ye saved through faith; and that not of yourselves: it is the gift of God:" Romans 10:9 says, "That if thou shalt confess with thy mouth the Lord Jesus, and shalt believe in thine heart that God hath raised him from the dead, thou shalt be saved." Our salvation comes through Faith in Christ and is secure. After they receive salvation, many people are satisfied with just going to heaven. You don't have to do anything else to make it into heaven. However, you don't work to be saved, you work *because you are saved*. In Matthew 25:35-36, Jesus said, "For I was an hungered, and ye gave me meat: I was thirsty, and ye gave me drink: I was a stranger, and ye took me in: Naked, and ye clothed me: I was sick, and ye visited me: I was in prison, and ye came unto me." These are the kinds of works we do because we are saved. Helping others, showing others kindness, and letting others see our light so they can glorify our Father in heaven. We don't do these things to get saved, we do them because we are saved. Therefore, God gives rewards for the Christian services we do toward others because we are saved.

The Bible speaks of several different crowns that God will give as a reward to His people when they get to heaven. The incorruptible crown will be received by all of God's people (1 Corinthians 14:27). It's a crown that can't be tarnished or corroded; it won't fade, and it will be incorruptible. You will receive this crown because you stood up against temptations, against passions, and against lust. When you didn't feel like praying, you denied your feelings and prayed anyway. When you didn't feel like fasting, you denied yourself and fasted anyway. When you didn't feel like praising God, you lifted up your hands and praised Him anyway. When you didn't feel like going to church, you denied yourself and went anyway. It is a crown of self-denial.

There is also a crown of righteousness (2 Timothy 4:8). It is a crown to those Christians who endured a lot of suffering and persecution for the cause of Christ, fought the good fight of faith, and were anxious to see Jesus Christ's second coming.

Then there is a crown of rejoicing (1 Thessalonians 2:19). Remember how excited you were when your favorite team won a game or something special happened in your life—how you jumped, shouted, and clapped for joy? When you see Jesus Christ and are in His presence, nothing can be compared to His unspeakable joy. There will be no more crying, no more pain, no more sickness, no more disease or heartaches. There will be so much excitement and joy. We'll be able to see our loved ones who have passed on before us in the Lord—some friends, maybe neighbors, and others we had met on earth who made it to the kingdom. We'll be able to see Adam—God's first man—Abraham, David, Moses and all the patriots of old. We'll see Peter and Paul and the rest of God's apostles. But, most importantly, we'll see Jesus

Christ, who shed His blood for us, and we'll see God Himself. What a day of rejoicing that will be!

There is also the crown of life (James 1:12, Revelation 2:10). This crown will be given to those who refused to deny Christ in a life-or-death situation. They would choose to die rather than deny Christ.

This reminds me of Stephen, a man full of faith and power. He was one of the seven men chosen by the apostles to handle the business of the church. Stephen did great wonders and miracles among the people. Some accused him of blasphemous words against Moses and God. They stirred the people up against him, and he was brought before the Sanhedrin court. Stephen spoke before the court with such power of the Holy Spirit against the unbelief of Israel that they gnashed on him with their teeth and stoned him. But before he died, he looked up and saw heaven open and the glory of God and Jesus standing on the right hand of God.

Then there are the ones who will go through the great tribulation, and the false prophets will give them a choice: to worship the Antichrist and live, or to worship Christ and die. Those who choose to worship Christ and are not afraid to give up their lives will be beheaded. They will be resurrected at the end, and God will give them the crown of life.

Now there is finally the crown of glory (1 Peter 5:4). This crown is given to those preachers, pastors, evangelists, teachers, and others who willingly fed the flock—not for money or prestige—and were a good example for the people. For "when the chief Shepherd (Jesus Christ) shall appear, ye shall receive a crown of glory that fadeth not away."

Chapter 10

The Tribulation

After the rapture has taken place, the Holy Spirit will also be removed from the earth. Nothing will hold Satan and his demons from spewing his unrestricted evil upon the earth.

The tribulation period will be a seven-year period when God will pour out His wrath upon the people for their rebellion and rejection of Him. He will allow Satan and his demons to cause severe suffering that has never been known to man to come upon the face of the earth.

God will allow the nation of Israel to suffer so intensely until they will finally confess that Jesus Christ is Lord. In the Book of Revelation, God revealed to the apostle John the three different kinds of judgments that He will pour out on man. Each kind of judgment will have seven demonstrations, and each one will become worse than the one before. The three different kinds of judgments will be the seal judgments, the trumpet judgments, and the vial judgments.

God's three series of judgements are introduced in Revelation: the seal judgements in Chapter 6, the trumpet judgements in Chapters 8 and 9, and the vial judgements in Chapters 15 and 16. The judgements will come upon the earth in different ways: deception, death, famine, and war, but Christ is sovereign in every part.

The tribulation starts after Jesus Christ the Lamb <u>opens the first</u> of seven seals. We read in Revelation 6:1-2, "And I saw when the Lamb opened one of the seals, and I heard, as it were the noise of thunder, one of the four beasts saying, Come and see. And I saw, and behold a white horse: and he that sat on him had a bow; and a crown was given unto him; and he went forth conquering, and to conquer." Do not confuse this rider on this white horse with the one in Revelation 19:11-16, which is the King of kings.

The rider that sat on the horse in Revelation 6:1-2 is the Antichrist. He begins a series of terrible events. He will come in deception, imitating Christ and claiming to be Him. The people will have itching ears, not wanting to know the truth. The Antichrist will go forth, conquering until he has control over the entire world—not through war, but through deception and manipulation.

This will be the beginning of the Antichrist's coming into power that had been prophesied by the prophet Daniel (Daniel 7:2-7). The Antichrist's power will come from Satan. "And the beast which I saw was like unto a leopard, and his feet were as the feet of a bear, and his mouth as the mouth of a lion: and the dragon gave him his power, and his seat, and great authority" (Revelation 13:12). He comes first as a peacemaker with great influence. He will be an eloquent speaker, speaking with authority, and will be very convincing and politically savvy. The whole world will admire him, and he will become the political leader of the entire world.

When the Antichrist comes into power, the world will be in chaos and looking for peace. There will still be terrorism, fire, hurricanes, racial conflicts, financial conflicts, and wars between nations. Israel and middle eastern countries will still be at odds over their lands. It will be a time when people will be easily deceived because the Holy Spirit is no longer on the earth to lead them.

Through his brilliance, the Antichrist will be able to solve the unsolvable problem between Israel and the Middle East for the first time in hundreds of years. He will make a covenant with Israel to protect them and allow them to rebuild their long-awaited temple and restore their feast (Daniel 9:27). They will admire him, for he will accomplish something that no other man over hundreds of years has been able to do. Finally, Israel will seemingly have peace.

But it is false peace. For three-and-a-half years, Israel will be deceived by the Antichrist before his true character comes to the surface.

SEE REVELATION 6:3

The second seal will be opened, which is a symbol of war. The Antichrist will be given power to take peace from the earth. Violence will become a common thing. People will be killing one another through assassinations, revolts, and massacres. Things will get worse by the day.

SEE REVELATION 6:5

The third seal will be opened and bring famine into the world. With a scarcity of food, prices will skyrocket, food lines will be common, and food will be rationed and measured. People will die from hunger because of lack of food for their families and children.

SEE REVELATION 6:7

The fourth seal will be opened, and this seal represents death. Power will be given to him to kill one fourth of the people on the earth. Death will be brought through slayings and hunger. The only help will be to turn to God and serve Him. Yet many will still refuse. I don't know how that many people will be destroyed, but nuclear weapons may be one theory.

SEE REVELATION 6:9

The <u>fifth seal</u> will be opened, which represents the souls that were slain for the Word of God. All the ones who stand up against the Antichrist will be martyred as a result. The Word of God tells us that whosoever shall lose their life for Christ's sake shall find it, and whosoever shall save his life shall lose it. This is why it is so important for God's people to know His Word. The prophet Hosea said, "My people are destroyed for lack of knowledge" (Hosea 4:6). And Jesus said, "Ye do err, not knowing the scripture, nor the power of God" (Matthew 22:29). Things will be so bad that if you don't know God's Word, you will give in to Satan.

SEE REVELATION 6:12

The <u>sixth seal</u> will be opened, and it represents anarchy, which is complete absence of government, violence, political disorder, and lawlessness. Just when you think things couldn't get any worse, they do. Great earthquakes will cause the mountains to move, and islands also will move out of their places. Chunks of the stars of heaven will fall upon the earth. People will try to hide themselves in the rocks of the mountains. Some will cry out to the mountains to fall on them as they will try to hide from God who sits on the throne. Who shall be able to stand? God will raise up 144,000 Jewish men (Revelation 7:4), all of whom have never been defiled by a woman (Revelation 14:4), and they will be sealed by God to evangelize the earth and preach the gospel of the kingdom to the people. Many will turn to God, but many will also reject him and be destroyed by the Antichrist.

SEE REVELATION 8:1

The <u>seventh seal</u> is opened next, and it will bring silence in heaven. Out of the seventh seal come the seven trumpet judgments. Revelation 8 and 9 tell us about the trumpet judgements. The first four trumpet judgments will greatly affect the land, salt water, fresh water, and heavenly bodies. Let us see how it will happen.

SEE REVELATION 8:7

When the angel sounds the <u>first trumpet</u>, hail and fire mingled with blood will be cast down upon the earth, and a third part of all trees and all green grass will be burnt up. There will be raging fires burning up vegetation, and the oxygen that the vegetables and the green trees provide will be gone, greatly affecting human life.

SEE REVELATION 8:8

When the <u>second trumpet</u> is sounded, a great mountain burning with fire will be cast into the sea, and a third part of it turned to blood. One third of all the creatures in the sea, including whales and sharks, will die. Also, one third of the ships will be destroyed. All the products and cargo that the ships carry will be destroyed and affect all nations.

SEE REVELATION 8:10

When the angel sounds the <u>third trumpet</u>, a great star from heaven will burn as it were a lamp and fall into the waters on one third part of the rivers and upon the fountains of water. A third part of the fresh water will become as bitter wormwood, and many men will die of the water because they were made bitter. The lack of healthy water to drink will cause sickness and disease.

SEE REVELATION 8:12

The <u>fourth trumpet</u> sounds, and the heavenly bodies affect the whole earth. One third of the sun, one third of the stars, and one third of the moon will be smitten and darkened. Can you imagine how dark the world will be through such a lack of light? This great disruption in the sky will cause one third less energy on earth and affects life. It will cause plant and animal life to die. Things will become worse than people have ever known, and things will still get worse. Listen to what the apostle John saw in Revelation 8:13: "And I beheld, and heard an angel flying through the midst of heaven, saying with a loud voice, woe, woe,

woe, to the inhabitants of the earth by reason of the other voices of the trumpet of the three angels, which are yet to sound." More grief, sorrow, trouble, and great misery will come.

SEE REVELATION 9:1

The fifth angel sounds the fifth trumpet, and surely things get worse. Each judgment will be more devastating than the last one. Here an angel falls from heaven and is given the key to the bottomless pit. The bottomless pit is the place where some demons are stored, the place where Satan will be imprisoned for one thousand years during the millennial period. The angel with the key will open the bottomless pit, and the smoke will darken the sun and the air.

Out of the pit will come locusts upon the face of the earth, and they will be given power as a scorpion. They will be instructed not to hurt the grass or any green thing or any trees, but only those men who did not have the seal of God on their foreheads.

The locusts will be instructed not to kill men, but they will torment them for five months. I've heard people who were stung by a bee say how painful it was, but the sting from the locusts will be so painful that men will seek death yet won't be able to find it. Death will flee from them. Can you imagine being tormented so badly and you can't get help, can't die, and must live in pain?

These locusts are not like the regular locusts we know of today, but these locusts come fit for battle. They are described as like unto a horse; they have a face as a man, hair as a woman, a crown like gold on their heads, teeth like a lion and a breastplate of iron. They have tails like scorpions with the power in them to make their stings last five months. This is the first woe.

SEE REVELATION 9:13

The sixth trumpet is sounded, and a voice speaks to the sixth angel to loose four angels that are bound. The very fact that these angels are bound indicates to me they are fallen angels prepared to slay one third of the men. Revelation 9:16-18 tells us that there will be an army of two hundred thousand thousand horsemen, and by this a third part of men will be slain—by fire, smoke, and brimstone that is issued out of their mouths. It will be horrifying. The rest of the men who were not killed will refuse to repent and turn to God. They would rather continue in their sins of idolatry, murder, sexual sins, witchcraft, and their other sins than to turn to God. When the midpoint of the tribulation comes, the Antichrist will break the covenant he made with Israel to protect them from their enemies, and he will invade the temple he had allowed them to build and begin to assault and persecute the Jews. The Gentiles will take over Jerusalem.

God then sends two witnesses from heaven for three-and-a-half years to prophesy and call the people to repentance. Some theologians say these two witnesses are Moses and Elijah. Moses had been buried by God Himself, and no one ever knew where he was buried. God sent a chariot and translated Elijah in a whirlwind to heaven. They will be back to preach to the people to turn to God.

God will give them power to accomplish the mission He placed before them. They will have power to shut the heaven and stop the rain. They will have power to turn water into blood and to smite the earth with plagues. No one will be able to harm them or kill them until their mission is accomplished.

After they have finished their mission, the Antichrist will make war against them, and God will allow the two witnesses to be killed. Their bodies will lie in the streets of Jerusalem for three-and-a-half days, and no one will bury them. My theory is through television cameras and satellites, the whole world will see their dead bodies lying in the streets of Jerusalem.

People who have rejected God will rejoice to see them dead and make fun and mock and be merry, sending gifts to each other and celebrating their death because they say that the two witnesses tormented them.

After they have been lying in the streets for three-and-a-half days, the Spirit of God will enter their dead bodies and bring them back to life, and they will stand up. When the people see them rise from the dead, they will become very fearful. Then a voice from heaven will speak to the waters and tell them to come up hither; and they will ascend to heaven in a cloud.

The earth will begin to shake, and a great earthquake will come. One tenth of Jerusalem will fall from the earthquake, and seven thousand men will be destroyed. This is the second woe.

SEE REVELATION 11:15

The <u>seventh trumpet</u> will sound. This is the third woe. The trumpet and great voices in heaven will say, "The kingdoms of this world are become the kingdoms of our Lord, and of his Christ; and he shall reign for ever and ever" (Revelation 11:15). This announcement by the seventh angel indicates that God is preparing to take over this world and Christ Jesus will reign for ever and ever.

War in Heaven

Satan now realizes that his time is short. He gathers his angels together to fight against God once again. "And there was war in heaven. Michael and his angels fought against the dragon; and the dragon fought and his angels, and prevailed not; neither was their place found any more in heaven. And the great dragon was cast out, that old serpent, called the Devil, and Satan, which deceiveth the whole world: he was cast out into the earth, and his angels were cast out with him" (Revelation 12:7-9).

Satan and his followers have been cast out of heaven, and there is "woe to the inhabitants of the earth and of the sea for the devil is come down unto you, having great wrath, because he knoweth that he hath but a short time" (Revelation 12:12). At this moment, God is now preparing to take over the government of this world.

False Prophet

The Bible speaks of another beast that comes out of the earth. This beast is the false prophet (Revelation 13:11-13). The false prophet will be the religious leader for the Antichrist and will turn people toward openly worshipping the Antichrist. He will turn the people to a false religion and will work hand-in-hand with the Antichrist. The false prophet will deceive many who dwell on earth by performing signs, wonders, and miracles in front of the people. He will cause fire to come down out of heaven, and he will deceive thousands.

The false prophet will tell the people on earth that they should make an image of the beast (Antichrist) that had been wounded by a sword and lived. The false prophet "had power to give life unto the image of the beast, that the image of the beast should both speak, and cause that as many as would not worship the image of the beast should be killed" (Revelation 13:15).

The false prophet will encourage the people to accept the mark of the beast. He will cause both small and great, rich and poor, free and bond to receive the mark in their right hand or in their forehead: "And that no man might buy or sell, except he that has the mark, or the name of the beast, or the number of his name. Here is wisdom. Let him that hath understanding count the number of the beast: for it is the number of a man; and his number is six hundred threescore and six" (666) (Revelation 13:17-18).

Can you imagine the suffering, the fear, and the stress that will come upon the people? Anyone who does not accept the mark of the beast will not be able to buy food for their family, purchase utilities for their home, or put gas in their car. Nothing can be purchased without the mark—not even necessities, such as health care.

By refusing to accept the mark of the beast, they will be destroyed by the Antichrist, and many will be beheaded. All these who accept the mark of the beast will confirm to Satan that they belong to him. The wrath of God will destroy them, and they will spend eternity in the lake of fire with Satan. Those who lose their lives for the cause of Christ will gain and save their lives. They will be resurrected to reign with Jesus Christ for a thousand years in His kingdom on earth. Revelation 7:13-14 tells us, "And one of the elders answered, saying unto me, What are these which are arrayed in white robes? and whence came they? And I said unto him, Sir, thou knowest. And he said to me, These are they which came out of great tribulation, and have washed their robes, and made them white in the blood of the Lamb."

In Revelation 16, God gets ready to end Satan's dominance over the earth by providing the vials of wrath upon the earth. Revelation 16:1 tells us that Apostle John said, "And I heard a great voice out of the temple saying to the seven angels, Go your ways and pour out the vials of the wrath of God upon the earth." The first angel poured a vial and a noisome and grievous sore fell upon the men which had the mark of the beast, and upon them which worshipped his image. The second angel poured the vial upon the sea, and it became as the blood of dead men: and every living soul died in the sea. The third angel poured the vial upon the river and fountains of water; and they became as blood. The fourth angel poured the vial upon the sun, and power was given into him to scorch men with fire. The fifth angel poured the vial upon the seat of the beast: and his kingdom was full of darkness; and they gnawed their tongues for pain. The sixth angel poured the vial upon the great river Euphrates; and the waters dried up. I can't imagine a person going through all this agony and still refuse to repent and turn to God. Some theologians believe that the purpose of the water drying up is to prepare the way of the Kings of the East to come into Palestine to join with the Antichrist for the battle of Armageddon.

Revelation 16:17 tells us, "And the seventh angel poured out his vial into the air; and there came a great voice out of the temple of heaven, from the throne, saying, **It is done**."

Armageddon

Armageddon is the place where Christ destroys the armies of the beast and the false prophet. Armageddon is a battle for the control of Jerusalem. This is the time when God will bring the great tribulation to a close and the reign of the Antichrist to an end. And the apostle John saw three unclean spirits like frogs come out of the mouth of the dragon (the devil) and out of the mouth of the beast (Antichrist) and out of the mouth of the false prophet (Revelation 16:13). They went forth throughout the whole world to kings to gather them for the battle against the almighty God. And they gathered them together into a place called Armageddon. There were voices, thunder and lightning and a great earthquake never before known to man. The island fled away, and the mountains could not be found. Hail fell from heaven, and every stone had the weight of a talent and fell upon men. Men blasphemed God and would not repent.

John saw heaven opened and a white horse; and he that sat upon him was called Faithful and True, and in righteousness he doth judge and make war and he had a name written, that no man knew, but he himself. And he was clothed with a vesture dipped in blood: and his name is called the Word of God. And he had on his vesture and on his thigh a name written, King of kings and Lord of lords (Revelation 19:11,13).

John also saw an angel standing in the sun, and he cried out with a loud voice to the fowl that fly in the midst of heaven and invited them to come and eat the flesh of kings and captains, mighty men, horses and the flesh of men free and bond, both small and great (Revelation 19:16).

The beast (the Antichrist) was taken, and with him the false prophet who had performed miracles before him and deceived them that had received the mark of the beast and them that worshipped his image. The Antichrist and the false prophet both were cast alive into a lake of fire burning with brimstone (Revelation 19:20). There they will spend eternity, in full consciousness, and burn in the lake of fire forever. The armies will fall dead and the vultures descend and eat their flesh. An angel came down from heaven, having the key of the bottomless pit and a great chain in his hand. And he laid hold on the dragon, that old serpent, which is the Devil, and Satan, and bound him a thousand years; and cast him into the bottomless pit, and shut him up, and set a seal upon him, that he should deceive the nations no more, until the thousand years should be fulfilled (Revelation 20:1-3). The battle of Armageddon will be over.

CHAPTER 11

THE MILLENNIUM

The millennium is a period of time when Christ will establish his kingdom on earth for a thousand years. This will take place after the earth has been devastated with great destruction during the tribulation, and there must be a time of transition. Now the glorious reign of Christ will be established, and God will restore everything that has been messed up by sin and set all creation right again. It will be a perfect system, both politically and socially. People will be saved, and those who went through the tribulation will enter the millennium in their <u>natural bodies</u>. They will be able to procreate and have children and long lives. There will be a great multitude, which no man can number, of all nations, and kindreds, and people, and tongues standing before the throne and before the Lamb, clothed with white robes and palms in their hands. These are the ones who came out of the great tribulation and have washed their robes and made them white in the blood of the Lamb. They refused to deny Christ and worship the Antichrist and were martyred. They "were beheaded for the witness of Jesus, and for the Word of God, and which had not worshipped the beast, neither his image, neither had received his mark upon their foreheads, or in their hands; and they lived and reigned with Christ a thousand years" (Revelations 20:4).

The Lord shall be King over all the earth. "And the government shall be upon his shoulder: and his name shall be called

Wonderful, Counselor, The mighty God, The everlasting Father, The Prince of Peace" (Isaiah 9:6). Jerusalem will be the capital of the world. "And it shall come to pass, that every one that is left of all the nations which came against Jerusalem shall even go up from year to year to worship the King, the Lord of hosts, and to keep the feast of tabernacles" (Zechariah 14:16). This was a feast that lasted seven days. It commemorated the Jews wandering in the wilderness. The whole feast was a joyous time.

This is a glimpse of how it will be in the millennial kingdom. There will be no rain and no weeping; there will be great rejoicing in Jerusalem, and children will live to be a hundred years old (Isaiah 65:20). They will build houses and plant vineyards and enjoy the work of their hands. "They shall not labor in vain" (Isaiah 65:21-23). "The wolf and the lamb will feed together, the lion shall eat straw like the bullock, and the serpent shall feed on dust and shall not be able to hurt or destroy" (Isaiah 65:25). The people will have a pure language and speak the same thing as it was before God confused man's tongue back in the Tower of Babel days (Genesis 11:9). There will be no iniquity in people or people speaking lies. There will be no deceitful tongues and no evil anymore: there will be peace, joy, singing and praising the Lord and a full knowledge of the Lord. "The leopard shall lie down with the kid; the suckling child shall play on the hole of the asp, and the weaned child shall put his hand on the cockatrice' den (the most poisonous snake). They cannot and will not hurt or do any harm" (Isaiah 11:6-9). Can you imagine a child playing with a snake? There will be so much joy and rejoicing in the kingdom. Sometimes I wonder if these animals will be able to speak and understand, like the serpent in the Garden of Eden.

Revelation 20:7-8 tells us that when Satan is loosed, the thousand years will be over, and he will go out to deceive all the nations of earth. He will gather them together to battle, and it will be a number as the sand of the sea. The ones Satan gathers are those who survived the great tribulation and went into the millennial kingdom in their natural bodies. They gave birth to children who became the kingdom children, and they had the right to choose between Christ and Satan; but Satan, through his deception, convinced them to rebel against Christ and become part of his army to battle against God and try to overthrow him. "And they went up on the breadth of the earth, and compassed the camp of the saints about, and the beloved city: and fire came down from God out of heaven and devoured them. And the devil that deceived them was cast into the lake of fire and brimstone, where the beast and the false prophet are, and shall be tormented day and night for ever and ever" (Revelation 20:9-10).

White Throne Judgement

Now the day of reckoning has come to all those unbelievers who rejected God throughout all the ages. Now they must stand before God and be judged. This judgement is not the same as the judgement seat of Christ, who judged the believing saints after they had been raptured; this white throne judgment is for those who rejected God and Christ.

"There will be a great white throne. And the dead, small and great, will stand before God; and the books will be opened: and another book will be opened, which is the Book of Life: and the dead will be judged out of these things which are written in the book, according to their works. And the sea will give up the dead which are in it; and death and hell will deliver up the dead which are in them: and they will be judged every man according to their works. Death and hell will be cast into the lake of fire. This is the second death. And whosoever was not found written in the book of life will be cast into the lake of fire" (Revelation 20:11-15). "Then shall he say also unto them on the left hand, Depart from me, ye cursed, into everlasting fire, prepared for the devil and his angels" (Matthew 25:41). Jesus has put all enemies under His feet, including death.

CHAPTER 12

GOD'S PURPOSE FULFILLED

1 Corinthians 15:24 tells us, "Then cometh the end, when he shall have delivered up the kingdom to God, even the Father; when he shall have put down all rule and all authority and power." God's purpose is completed. Jesus Christ has turned the kingdom over to His Father. Now God has fulfilled His purpose for mankind that He ordained before the foundation of the world, to establish a heaven on earth for His children to live forever in eternity. "And I saw a new heaven and a new earth: for the first heaven and the first earth were passed away; and there was no more sea" (Revelation 21:1). "The former shall not be remembered, nor come into mind" (Isaiah 65:17).

Oh, how beautiful it will be! You can't even imagine it. "Eye hath not seen, nor ear heard, neither have entered into the heart of man, the things which God hath prepared for them that love him" (1 Corinthians 2:9). Revelation Chapter 21 describes the city. The apostle John in his vision saw the holy city, New Jerusalem, coming down from heaven. It was so beautiful that he described it as a bride adorned for her husband. As the great city, the holy Jerusalem, descended out of heaven, it showed the glory of God.

The city was so big. It was 1,500 miles long, 1,500 miles wide and 1,500 miles high. It was absolutely mind boggling. The city had a wall with twelve foundations, and each foundation was made of precious jewels. The first foundation was jasper; the second, sapphire; the third, chalcedony; the fourth, emerald; the fifth, sardonyx; the sixth, sardius; the seventh, chrysolyte; the eighth, beryl; the ninth, topaz; the tenth, chrysoprasus; the eleventh, jacinth; and the twelfth, amethyst.

I can't even imagine how beautiful that city will be. In the vision, the twelve foundations had the names of the twelve apostles of the Lamb. The city had a wall great and high at almost three hundred feet, and the building of the wall was jasper. There were twelve gates to the wall, and each gate was made of pearl. That's where we get the phrase "Pearly Gates," and the names of the twelve gates were the twelve tribes of the children of Israel. And the gates of it shall not be shut at all by day: for there shall be no night. And the city was pure gold, and the streets of the city were pure gold, as if it were transparent glass.

There is a pure river of the water of life, clear as crystal, proceeding out of the throne of God and of the Lamb. In the midst of the street and on either side of the river there was the tree of life, which bare twelve manners of fruits, and yielded her fruit every month: and the leaves of the tree were for the healing of the nations. And there shall be no more curse: but the throne of God and of the Lamb shall be in it; and His servants shall serve Him: and they shall see His face; and His name shall be in their foreheads. And there shall be no night there; and they need no candles, neither light of the sun; for the Lord God giveth them light: and they shall reign forever and ever. God himself will be there and dwell on His throne.

Oh, how great it's going to be when we all get to heaven. No more death, no more pain, no more sickness, no more worrying, no more broken hearts, no more tears, no more financial problems. It will be a place of eternal peace and unspeakable joy. God will have fulfilled His eternal purpose for man. The only way you can make it to that kingdom is to accept Jesus Christ as your Lord and Savior. Jesus said, "I am the way, the truth, and the life: no man cometh unto the Father but by me" (John 14:6). He gives everyone an open invitation to come to Him, and the ones who come to accept Him He will in no wise turn them down.

What would you give to live forever in the kingdom of God? There is absolutely nothing on earth that is worth losing your soul. We all love family, but not even a mother, father, husband, wife, or child whom you love so dearly are worth losing your soul. If you haven't already made the decision to accept Christ as your Savior, do it today. Romans 10:8 tells us, "That if thou shalt confess with thy mouth the Lord Jesus, and shalt believe in thine heart that God hath raised him from the dead, thou shalt be saved." Join us in the royal family of God. I hope to see you in that great, glorious city of God, where we will all live forever in His kingdom on earth.

God bless you, and may heaven smile upon you.

CPSIA information can be obtained
at www.ICGtesting.com
Printed in the USA
FFOW01n0334230618
47211165-49995FF